FOOTBALL CRAZY

Activity Book

All about me

This book belongs to..

I live at..

....

....

I am....13...... years old.

This is a picture of me in my football kit.

I support

My favourite football team is ..... ManU ....

My favourite players are ....

....

....

This is a picture of my favourite football team.

My team!

The friends I play football with are ....
....
....
....
....
....

We play together at ....

My favourite position is ....

This is a picture of my friends and me playing football.

It's a draw!

Can you make these 4 football players look exactly the same?

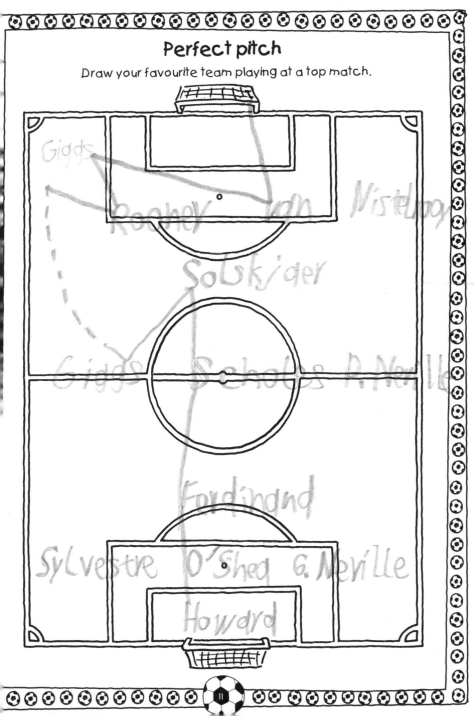

Kick off

The match is about to begin and the crowd are cheering the players onto the pitch. See how many of these things you can see.

scarves ☐   beards ☐   flags ☐

cameras ☐   bobble hats ☐   hot dogs ☐

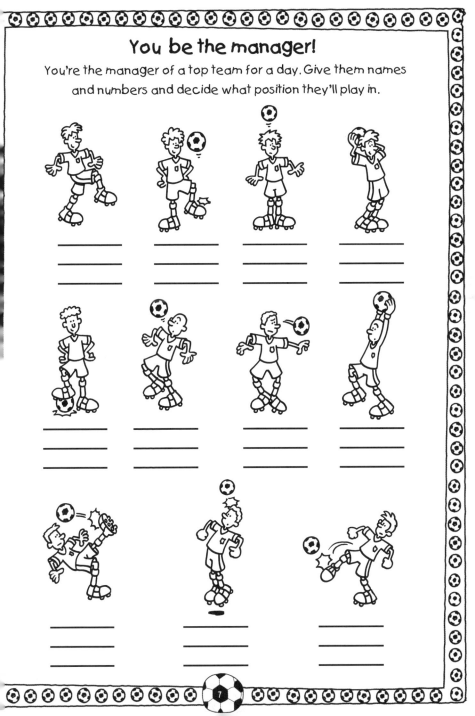

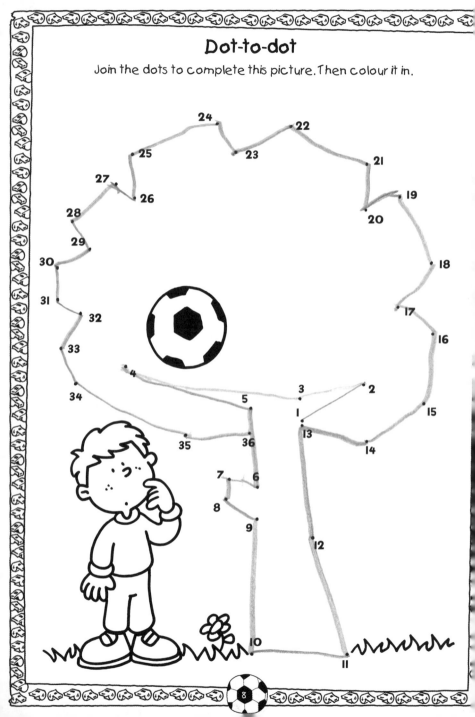

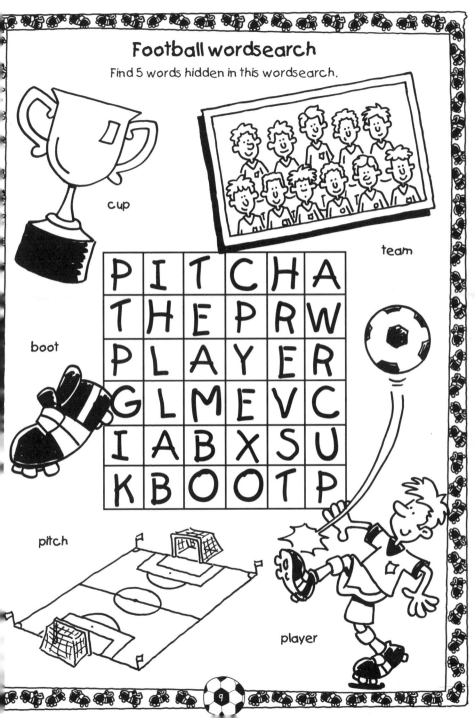

Complete the picture

Complete this picture by joining the dots.

Amazing maze

Help the player dodge his way through the maze to the goal.

Dear diary

Can you draw the correct times on these clocks?

Kick off was at 3 o'clock.

Half time was at 3.45.

The final whistle went at 4.45.

Missing words

Find the correct words to complete these sentences.

1. Goal, shouted the captain, as the **ball** hit the back of the net.

scarves

2. The fans waved their **scarves** when the team arrived.

cup

3. The referee blew his **whistle** at half time.

whistle

4. The captain held the **cup** high in the air.

net

5. The goal is also called a **net**.

ball

The management!

See if you can spot 5 differences between these 2 football managers.

Quick crossword

See if you can complete this crossword. Read the word clues, then look at the pictures for an extra helping hand.

Across
2. You wear this on your head.
3. These tighten your boots.
5. This is short for referee.

Down
1. You play football with this.
4. The referee might give you this.
6. A football supporter.

Free kick

Colour in this picture.

What's hiding?

Shade in the shapes that have a dot in them to reveal the hidden picture.

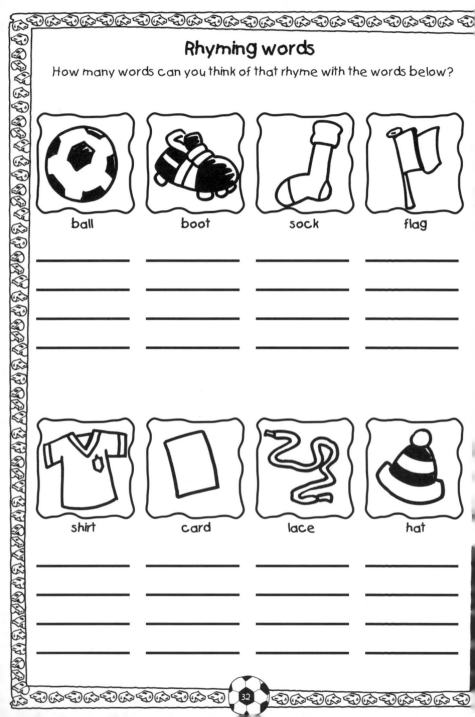

Jumbled jigsaw

Complete the jigsaw by drawing in the missing pieces.

Game on!

Yippee! Someone's scored a goal.

Which number player has hurt his leg?

Which player has scored?

What number is the goalie?

Odd one out

Which of these players is the odd one out?

Copy cat

Use the grid to copy this football fan. Then colour him in.

Winning team

Colour in the picture, then answer the questions below.

How many players are running?

How many players are standing still?

How many goals have been scored altogether?

Beginning with b

How many words that begin with the letter b can you see in this picture?

Picture sums

See how quickly you can complete these picture sums.

Football squares

Use the grid to enlarge this picture of a football cup.

Scrambled grid

Draw in the missing sections using the grid as a guide.

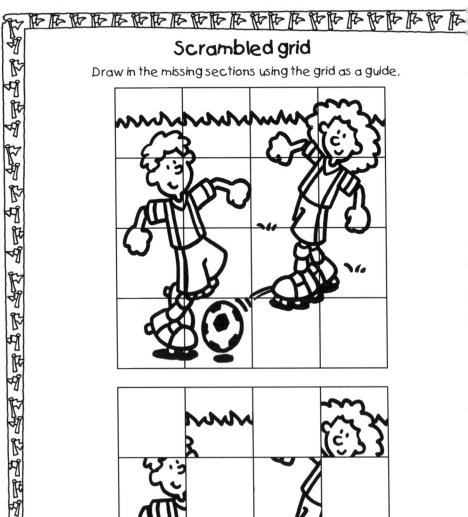

Half time

It's half time and the players are having a rest.
See if you can count these things.

How many players are drinking?

How many players are standing up?

How many players are sitting down?

Oh, ref!

The ref is about to give a card. Spot 5 differences between the 2 scenes.

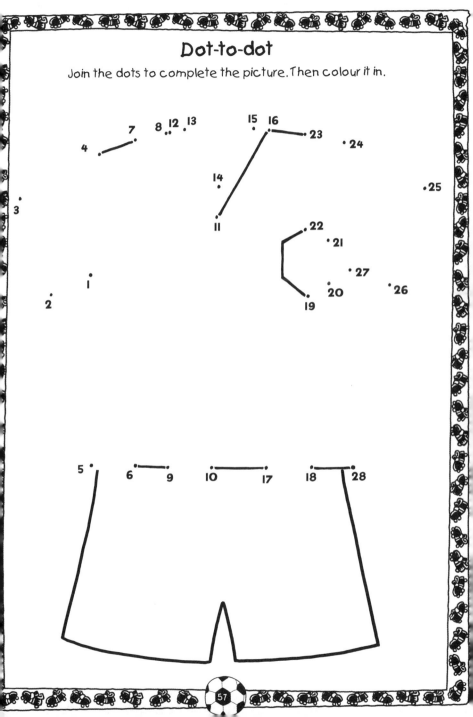

Football fan

See if you can spot the 5 differences between these 2 football fans.

Answers

Page 6

Page 9

Page 12
scarves - 7, beards - 2, flags - 5, cameras - 1, bobble hats - 7, hot dogs - 2.

Page 15

Page 19

Page 20

Page 23
The hidden number is 8.

Page 24
1. ball, 2. scarves, 3. whistle, 4. cup, 5. net.

Answers

Page 25

Page 26

Across	Down
2. Hat	1. Ball
3. Laces	4. Card
5. Ref	6. Fan

Page 30

Page 32

Here are just a few ideas:
ball, tall, hall, call, small.
boot, root, hoot, toot, loot.
sock, rock, clock, dock, shock.
flag, bag, rag, gag, hag.
shirt, curt, dirt, hurt, pert.
card, hard, guard, lard, shard.
lace, case, face, pace, race.
hat, bat, cat, fat, mat.

Page 34

Page 36

Answers

Page 37
2 has hurt his leg.
8 has scored.
The goalie is number 1.

Page 38

Page 39
d is the odd one out, the stripe on the shirt is missing.

Page 46
4 players are running.
4 players are standing still.
6 goals have been scored.

Page 47
balloon, birds, boat, bench, bin, boy, ball, bag, bat, bottle, bee, bushes, boots.

Page 49
Q: If you have a referee in football, what do you have in bowls?
A: *Cornflakes.*

Q: Why did a footballer take a piece of rope onto the pitch?
A: *He was the skipper.*

Q: What is a goalkeeper's favourite snack?
A: *Beans on post.*

Q: What lights up a football stadium?
A: *A football match.*

Page 50

Page 52
Picture sums are: 5, 3, 6, 7, 4.

Answers

Page 55

3 players are drinking.

8 players are standing up.

3 players are sitting down.

Page 56

Page 60

Page 58

Page 59

8 - 2 = 6   7 + 4 = 11

3 + 5 = 8   4 - 3 = 1